Debbie GIBSON

Written by Gary Poole

Modern Publishing
A Division of Unisystems, Inc.
New York, New York 10022

Contents

One of Debbie's stops on her tour was Radio City Music Hall in New York City. Robin Platzer, Images

About Debbie Gibson

—Recording star at age seventeen.
—Debut album *Out of the Blue* sold 3 million copies.
—This yielded five top-five singles, including the No. 1 hit "Foolish Beat."
—Second album, *Electric Youth,* is better than the first and is moving rapidly up the charts.
—Debbie is wholesome, real, down-to-earth.
—Junior version of Olivia Newton-John and Karen Carpenter with a dash of Madonna dance pop.
—Debbie receives 5,000 fan letters a week.
—Epitomizes the sound of young America —bouncy, exuberant and striving for success.
—Quote: "I'm glad I can show kids that you don't have to dye your hair purple to be a pop musician."

Debbie likes being a teenager. She labels herself as "clean-cut, yet funky." AP/Wide World Photos

Introduction

How does a young girl become a top recording star at age seventeen? Like the man said, "She *earned* it!"

That's exactly what Debbie Gibson did, and it took all of her seventeen years to make it to the top.

No overnight success or bolt of lightning flashed and transformed Debbie, the teenage girl-next-door, into the smash hit that she is today. Debbie has been working at being a performer since she was three!

The press has dubbed her "a junior Madonna," then added the creaminess of Olivia Newton-John and the all-American wholesomeness of Karen Carpenter. Quite a combination! And it's all wrapped up in Debbie Gibson.

Since signing with Atlantic Records two years ago, Debbie, now eighteen, has surprised the so-called "smart guys" of the record industry in many ways. Her first album, *Out of the Blue,* sold three million copies, and out of that came five top-five singles, including the No. 1 hit "Foolish Beat"!

As if that wasn't enough to set the executives' heads spinning, Debbie also wrote, produced, arranged and performed her own songs. As a result, she is the youngest pop star ever to accomplish all four tasks for a No. 1 record. There aren't many female producers in the record business, so when Debbie came along she became the first *teen-age* female producer ever.

On the heels of that success, Debbie followed up with her second album, *Electric Youth,* which turned out to be an even more polished collection of her own original pop tunes.

Electric Youth is a peppy little anthem in which Debbie celebrates her own generation. "It points out that it's not unusual to expect good things from young people," Debbie said in an interview. "Look at the fifteen and sixteen-year-olds who are out there winning Olympic gold medals. I just couldn't see what the big deal was about my age when my first record was released."

Where did this confident success with the flashing smile come from? Is she what she appears to be—just an average teen-ager? How is all this glamour affecting her life? Debbie Gibson is riding the crest of an awesome success. Read on.

Since she was three years old, Debbie's parents always have encouraged her special talent. Robin Platzer, Images

The Early Years

She was always a musical child. As an infant, even her gurgling sounded good! Of course, no one paid *that* the slightest attention, but she was pleasant to listen to. Her parents didn't think there was anything special going on. Later, they would discover that their little Deborah had been born with perfect pitch!

When Debbie began playing the piano by ear at the age of three, her parents really took notice. By the age of four she had picked out her first tune on the keyboard. It was the 1974 hit, "Billy, Don't Be a Hero." You can bet Debbie's parents made sure everyone who came to see them got to hear that!

With typical modesty, Debbie gives her parents all the credit. "My mother's got a really good ear," she said, "and my dad used to sing with a barbershop quartet, called The Peanuts, when he was fourteen. He and the three other guys were orphans in a home for boys. They did TV and toured with Bob Hope."

Enthusiasm could be Debbie's middle name. "I always wanted to get my hands into everything," she said. If she saw a play, she wanted to be in it, or a TV commercial, even an opera, *that* was where she visualized herself.

There is an old saying that if you visualize in your mind what you want to be, it will become easier for you to achieve. If that is true, then Debbie Gibson is certainly living proof of it.

As far back as she can remember, Debbie has known what she's wanted to be. It's a goal from which she has not strayed, not even the slightest. She even wrote her first song while in kindergarten!

The name of that song was "Make Sure You Know Your Classroom," and it goes like this: Make sure you know your classroom/Make sure you know your seat/I'll help you find your teacher/I hope she looks so sweet.

How did she go about writing that song at such a young age? Debbie recalls, "I can remember sitting on a couch, all scrunched up, figuring out each note by ear and then writing it down."

Talk about painstaking! It just goes to show that even in kindergarten she was a hard worker. That's the way it all began, and the amazing thing is—that's the way she composes today.

The old saying "children should be seen and not heard" was never used in Debbie's family. Even at age three, Debbie stood in front of the Christmas tree and sang carols for family and friends. It seems you can't stop Debbie from singing any more than you can prevent the sun from rising in the East.

Up until the age of five, Debbie continued to play the piano by ear. Then Debbie's parents decided she should take her music seriously. So they took Debbie to a piano teacher, Martin Estrin. He was her teacher for several years, and just happens to be the man who taught piano to her idol—Billy Joel!

When it came time to further her education, Debbie attended public school in Merrick, New York. During elementary school, she was placed in a program for gifted children while she kept up with her regular classes.

It was during this program that she wrote her own half-hour musical entitled *Alice in Operaland*. The plot of that concerns a young girl who meets up with storybook characters who all sing to her.

Although she took her "serious" music seriously, Debbie was no square. Often she would take her classical piano pieces and "rock them up" just for fun. Her teacher may have frowned on this, but at the same time realized where her destiny lay. It was just another example of how her creativity was just bursting to get through.

The unspoiled teen star was brought up in suburban Merrick, where she lives with the kind of close-knit family that, as her Italian-American mother puts it, "has macaroni on Sunday or it's just not Sunday."

And what a family! She has three sisters: Denise, who is fourteen and still in high school; Karen, twenty-two, her oldest sister, who recently graduated from Vassar College; and Michele, twenty-one, who is now attending Vassar College.

Debbie considers her folks "the greatest." "Our family is a team. We all work together, and that's what it takes," said Debbie. "You need a good team that

Debbie and her three sisters—(l-r) Michele, Denise and Karen— attend Atlantic Records' 40th anniversary party at Madison Square Garden last May. Robin Platzer, Images

Although Debbie works hard juggling both school and a career, she still finds time to enjoy being a teenager. Judie Burstein/ Photoreporters

believes in you to get anywhere."

Debbie knows she could never have done it alone. Teamwork. It's what got her started, and it's what keeps her going today.

In high school, Debbie managed to make the honor roll and perform constantly. How did she juggle school and a career at the same time?

"I just made a schedule and stuck by it," said Debbie. "I had a certain time to do certain things—like usually I'd take my classes in the morning and finish school by noon. Then I would go home, do my homework FIRST, so I wouldn't have to worry about it anymore. That would leave the rest of the afternoon and evening to work on my songs in the studio." Debbie added, "Fortunately, I'm a quick learner, and I tried to be a good student."

Debbie's favorite subject was Spanish. She took it for five years and hopes someday to be able to record albums in foreign languages.

When reporters asked the kids at school to describe Debbie they answered: "A really nice girl," and "cool," or "she's not stuck-up."

When the same reporters asked Debbie about the kids at school, she replied,

Debbie's wardrobe ranges from a large selection of sweatsuits and jeans to miniskirts and formal dresses. Judie Burstein/ Photoreporters

"There are three types of reactions I get. Some ask for autographs, some resent what I do. Then there are my friends."

Her friends are still with her. Sometimes when she gets back from a tour, she likes to get together with them at someone's house and just talk. "Sometimes we get loud!" she grins.

Where does Debbie get the inspiration for all the songs she writes? "I've always taken anything surrounding me and put it to creative use," said Debbie. "When I'm out with friends, if I hear an idea, a catchy phrase, I turn it into a song."

It's just that simple. Of course, it takes talent and imagination to draw upon everyday situations and use them creatively.

As Debbie changes, her music changes, too. Her lyrics are becoming less clichéd, although they remain straightforward.

When asked if she minds fans approaching her, Debbie replies: "I'm honored. It's nice to know that people like what I do."

Debbie has become a role model for young girls across America. Of course, she didn't plan it that way. "I'm just myself," Debbie added. "I wear what I like."

What Debbie likes is an interesting array of clothing, such as jeans, high-cut baggies, form-fitting stonewashed jeans, black miniskirts, and bright-colored leggings. She has tons of T-shirts along with denim jackets which she decorated herself.

Debbie likes to mix and match sweatshirts. She also likes clothes big and baggy, especially sweaters. "They feel comfortable," she said, "and they make me comfortable, too."

Anyone who wants to have the Debbie Gibson look will need sneakers, high-tops or running shoes and black flats, which are basic and good for walking, dancing or just looking good.

She loves hats, too, and baggy jackets in all different colors and patterns. On occasion, Debbie wears suspenders and tie-up boots.

"I love rolled-up pants with no socks and flat shoes. I just like to look colorful," Debbie added. "Although sometimes I'll wear white when I want to look classy."

In short, Debbie wants to project herself as a clean-cut, funky teenager. Which is exactly what she is. "I think being hip is looking comfortable with what you are. You are 'with it' when you look comfortable in your clothes. My image is …fun!" said Debbie.

The Big Break

How do you make it big in show business? Are some people just so talented that they cannot be ignored? Sometimes that is the case, but more often than not luck plays a major role in whether someone does or doesn't make it to the top. It's called "The Big Break". Stars are constantly being asked, "Who gave you your first big break? How did you get started?"

There is truth to the old saying, "You have to be in the right place at the right

Debbie attributes most of her success to having a supportive mother and father. Judie Burstein/Photoreporters

time." We might add, "and meet the right people, those people who have the power to give you the opportunity to prove yourself."

Where did Debbie Gibson's "Big Break" come from? How did she get started? How did she get where she is today?

First of all, Debbie wouldn't have gotten anywhere if she hadn't had the full support of her family. Her mother and father supported her every step of the way, providing her with a home filled with love and warmth, and the priceless gift of encouragement.

From the time when she began picking out tunes on the piano, Debbie's parents knew she was something special. She would listen to the radio, then play what she had heard on the piano.

Seeing this, her parents began her classical piano training with Martin Estrin at age five.

She began writing little songs while still in kindergarten. By the time she was nine she was singing in nearby New York in the Metropolitan Opera Children's Chorus.

"People in charge always made a big deal about us kids talking to the artists," Debbie recalls, "but they were always so nice—Renata Scotto, Placido Domingo. The chorus had about fifty kids. When you auditioned for a specific opera, the director would have the words written out in whichever language it was in—Italian, Russian, French—and underneath, what they meant in English."

From this, Debbie discovered that she had a passion for languages. "I once did a show in Puerto Rico and spoke to four thousand people in Spanish, and they loved it!" said Debbie.

When she was twelve, her parents gave her a musical synthesizer. Debbie remembers, "It was the time of my confirmation. Everyone gets jewelry for their confirmation, but I told my mother that I wanted a synthesizer. I know that sounds silly, but that's what I really wanted!"

Once she got the synthesizer, Debbie was off and running. She entered a local radio station songwriting contest and promptly won first prize—one thousand dollars!

It then occurred to the family that she might have a future in songwriting. By now Debbie had written a lot of songs, but no one had any idea about how to get her songs heard by the so-called "right people."

Then her parents contacted an entertainment attorney, who soon had her playing her songs for professional studio musicians. This resulted in what is known in the music business as a "demo," or demonstration tape.

"At first it didn't sound the way I wanted it to," recalls Debbie. "I knew how I wanted it to sound in my head, but it wasn't coming out that way. So I played around with three little tape recorders and my synthesizer. I played one part into a tape recorder, then I'd play that back while I was taping a second part." She laughs, "By the end it was so fuzzy that you really couldn't hear anything!"

So the next step was inevitable. Her parents helped her set up her very own multitrack recording studio in their garage.

While all this was going on, Debbie was trying to get jobs acting in commercials. That did not come easy. Even though she managed to get an agent (she was now age eleven), it took a whole year of auditioning before she landed her first commercial.

Again, who helped her? Her mother—who drove her into the city after school to make the rounds of advertising agencies and attend all those auditions.

Along the way, Debbie had many disap-

Makeup artists prepare Debbie before she goes on stage. Judie Burstein/Photoreporters

pointments. She came close to signing a record deal six years ago, but didn't get one until, finally, Atlantic Records signed her up.

The producers told her to pick one of her songs and they'd make a single out of it. So she selected "Only in My Dreams." This was a song she had written when she was only fourteen years old and which, she said, only took fifteen minutes to write.

So the "Big Break" came. But it came only after all the preparation that went into it, and the loving, caring support that she received from her family. Her mother is now her personal manager, her oldest sister, Karen, helps take care of her sound system, and her other sister, Michele, designs a lot of her stage clothes. So it's a *family* success story, and one that certainly serves as an inspiration to us all.

Call it luck, hard work, dedication and determination. Or you can call it making your own luck and making *sure* you are in the right place at the right time. But whatever you call it, one thing is for sure: Debbie Gibson *deserves* to be the star that she is today. All her fans certainly agree on that!

Debbie was a featured guest with her mother on Joan Lunden's show. Also pictured here is Michael Kraus, Joan's husband.
Judie Burstein/Photoreporters

On Top

To say that Debbie Gibson has reached the top is putting it mildly. She's a girl who became a living legend at age eighteen! How many performers can say that? Michael Jackson can, and Judy Garland skyrocketed to fame around that age in *The Wizard of Oz*. However, the list of entertainers who reached the unreachable star at such an early age is very small indeed.

During an outdoor concert at Jones

On Debbie's eighteenth birthday she is presented with a special birthday cake at Ed Debevic's diner in Hollywood, CA. AP/Wide World Photos

Beach, NY, Debbie wowed her audience to their feet, clapping, screaming, and throwing teddy bears onstage. The concert alone grossed almost $200,000. Teddy bears decorate her bedroom at home, where approximately 5,000 fan letters arrive each week.

This kind of fame could turn the head of an average teenager, but not Debbie! She remains the same down-to-earth girl-next-door that she always was. "My image is that I have no image," says Debbie. "I'm just an everyday person."

With Debbie Gibson, what you see is what you get. "I am what I am," she said.

When she first signed with Atlantic Records, the people there said she had to come up with an image.

"They even thought I should look older!" exclaimed Debbie. "Imagine that! So I asked why. I pointed out that *guys* in the business don't have to have an image, and that's one reason why they get taken more seriously. Look at Billy Joel."

That was two years ago, and as grateful fans will testify, Debbie has stuck to her guns and let the "image makers" worry, while she just goes on being Debbie.

Her debut album, *Out of the Blue*, amazed the usually jaded record industry. It not

Debbie received a Gold Album for her debut album Out of the Blue. *After appearing on* The Morning Show, *Debbie takes the opportunity to have her picture taken with one of the show's hosts, Regis Philbin. Judie Burstein/Photoreporters*

only sold three million copies, but yielded five top-five singles. "Foolish Beat," as we all know, went on to become a No. 1 hit!

Then Atlantic Records released Debbie's second album, *Electric Youth*, which turned out to be an even more polished collection of original pop songs than *Out of the Blue*.

Debbie feels her music has grown from her first to her second album. "I'm happy with both, of course. *Out of the Blue*, since it was my first, will always hold a special place in my heart, but *Electric Youth* sounds more polished because we used a lot more live instrumentation. Therefore, I think it is a lot more human sounding than the first."

As on the first album, the songs on *Electric Youth* are simple, positive pop statements sung in Debbie's strong girlish voice. It points out that people should expect good things from young people.

Despite her many years studying the piano and her singing in the Metropolitan Opera Children's Chorus, Debbie's music contains no classical overtones.

"I think my classical training has had an impact on my music, no question about it," says Debbie. "You may not notice it, but it's there."

It's true. Rarely does anyone make it to the top in the record industry without a solid foundation and musical background. Debbie took the time to learn all that before moving into the pop arena. All of which proves that years of hard work went into the formation of the performer the world knows and loves today.

"Actually, it's because of my grounding in classical music that my music today has a definite direction," relates Debbie. She had to learn the more complicated music first, before she could compose and play the music she does now.

Debbie continues, "What I like about pop music is keeping it simple. Those are the best songs. I love the old Motown songs and four-chord rock-and-roll from the 1950s."

That's an interesting comment coming from a girl who was born in 1970. It simply proves that we all learn from the past, from the classical music of years ago to pop music. The trick is to know what to do with it. One thing is for sure—Debbie certainly knows.

Call it intuition, call it talent, but Debbie has taken all her training, all her hard work, and used it to zero in on her goal.

Being a celebrity is strange for Debbie because she still has her own idols and models. Being the everyday sort of girl she is, Debbie can't help going a little gaga when she meets a well-known rock singer or movie star. Along with Billy Joel, George Michael now ranks right up there in her eyes.

However, her other role models might surprise a lot of people. "I admire my mother and older sisters," said Debbie. "They are people I look up to and want to model myself after."

The Gibson family has always been close-knit. Her parents used to take Debbie and her sisters to rock concerts when they were younger. Then the four sisters would have a blast—dancing in the aisles.

It's this staying with her roots and remaining family oriented that probably accounts for Debbie's amazing popularity. Her fans feel: "She's one of us!"

Debbie's songs are also making it to the movies. One can be heard on the soundtrack of Whoopi Goldberg's *Fatal Beauty*, and another was scheduled for Michael J. Fox's *Bright Lights, Big City*.

Although her family and friends call her Deborah, she uses Debbie professionally. "They wind up calling me that, anyway," said Debbie. "When people ask my name, I say Deborah, because that's what it is and

Fame has not changed Debbie. She considers herself an "everyday person" just like everyone else. Robin Platzer, Images

Debbie's sister Michele, who is currently attending college, designs a lot of Debbie's stage clothes. Judie Burstein/ Photoreporters

Debbie comes from a close-knit family. Her sister Denise and their mom have some fun on Debbie's bike. Judie Burstein/ Photoreporters

John Gallegher, who appeared in the video Lost In Your Eyes, *jokes around with Debbie during a break. Judie Burstein/ Photoreporters*

Even though Debbie is a celebrity, she still will take out her camera when she sees one of her idols, such as Billy Joel or George Michael. Judie Burstein/Photoreporters

*The secret behind Debbie's success is that she has always had a
goal, even since she was a little girl. Judie Burstein/
Photoreporters*

what I've been called all my life, and two seconds later they turn around and call me Debbie!" So she decided, if you can't lick 'em, join 'em.

Debbie is as protective of her family as they are of her. "When people say to my mom now, 'Are you surprised that your daughter is having some success?' it annoys me because my family has been working just as hard as I have. You could have a super-talented person with all the ambition in the world, but you need people who believe in you to get anywhere."

The realities of the music world don't faze Debbie. "Ninety-five percent of the people I've met have been really nice," she says. "Some singers and groups are only interested in signing autographs and being photographed. But the people who are really good at what they do work hard."

Despite all her success and fame, with fans clamoring for her autograph, Debbie has kept her perspective. "In the beginning, people were worried about what to do with me," Debbie explains. "I just kept saying that we've got Madonna, we've got the glamorous Whitney Houston. The all-American teenage girl is the one that's missing right now—and it's me. I'm very clean-cut. I don't drink. I don't smoke. If I'm tired, I'm not going to use anything to make myself not tired—I'm going to take a nap."

This is one of the reasons why Debbie has become a top role model for young women across the nation. She points the way toward a decent life. She has proven that you can become a star and remain true to yourself and that in the fast lane of show business a performer does not have to use alcohol or take drugs to "fit in."

"I come from a level-headed, down-to-earth family with a basic Italian back-ground—home remedies and chicken soup. We go to church every week and we have macaroni every Sunday," she said with a smile.

With that sort of background, it's no won-der Debbie falls back on it when the going gets rough. It's her strength, her rock.

Why are Debbie Gibson's songs so popular? The reason is simple. They are all about teen romance and strike home to teenagers because the lyrics are about problems that concern them.

Some sample lyrics—ON UNREQUITED LOVE: Can't you see I'm not fooling nobody/ Don't you see the tears are falling down my face. ABOUT BREAKING UP: Oh, and I'll tell you boy it just isn't right/I won't say good-bye without a fight. GOING ALL THE WAY: I

Although Debbie has never had a steady boyfriend, she has
many male friends. One of them is heartthrob Brian Bloom.
Robin Platzer, Images

know your love could quench my desire/I know your love would light me on fire. *NOT GOING ALL THE WAY:* Nothing major ever happened/But it's the greatest feeling I've ever had.

So far, in her lifetime, Debbie has written over 300 songs about teenage romance and Debbie has never even gone steady.

You might ask, How can she write about all this without ever having had a steady boyfriend? The answer is observation. She's had years of watching her older sisters going through everything from puppy love to mature love to breakups and heartaches.

Combine that with her own personal feelings and sensitivity, not to mention a natural talent for writing, and you have the makings of a songwriter! So those heart-boggling insights are deep inside Debbie, because she's seen it all happen.

How did she find time to write, sing and record while she was going through school?

"I compose anywhere, anytime," Debbie answers. "If I hear a catchy phrase, I simply excuse myself and jot it down. Later on, I can work it up into a song."

She writes both the lyrics and music for a number in approximately fifteen minutes. Sometimes it takes a bit longer. She

Teddy bears decorate the Gibson home. Debbie received this oversized teddy bear as a present on her eighteenth birthday. Judie Burstein/Photoreporters

scribbles ideas on whatever is available at the moment, which she then jams carelessly into her pockets.

A comedian recently observed, "A songwriter could get rich just picking up the fallout from Debbie's pockets!"

Fortunately, none of it falls out. It remains snug in Debbie's pocket so that when she returns to the inner sanctum of her own home, she can quietly sit down and make sense out of her scribblings. Quite often, these hastily written notes will turn out to be worth putting into a song.

"Foolish Beat" is one such example. It was one of Debbie's early quickies. It reached the top of the charts and made her the youngest solo singer ever to write, produce and perform a No. 1 hit. It is included in her debut album, *Out of the Blue.*

Photographs often show the bubble-gum bard as part Lolita, part Shirley Temple, usually posed beside a cuddly stuffed teddy bear. Debbie loves stuffed teddy bears and her bedroom is filled with them. They can be seen piled on her bed, resting on double shelves above her desk, and even perched on the cornice above her window!

Although she graduated from high school with honors, Debbie is not headed for college. That may come later, but right

According to Debbie, one of the good things about being on the road is that it's energizing to appear on stage before a live audience. Judie Burstein/Photoreporters

now she has more immediate goals to attain.

There is a screenplay in the works for a romantic comedy, which she hopes to star in. One of her biggest ambitions has been to become a movie star. The way things are going, it looks like that could happen. After all, she has had a variety of experiences acting in commercials, and she knows her way around a camera.

Debbie also would love to work with Billy Joel and George Michael. She did appear on stage with Billy Joel once. He heard she was in the audience and simply invited her up on stage.

"I want to keep the funness and youthfulness of my music," she said. "If it's fun for me, then hopefully, it'll be fun for the audience."

Debbie need not worry. It's always fun whenever she performs, and everyone has a good time. After all, that's what entertaining is all about.

One of the strange things about being a teenage success is that Debbie finds herself underage at most of the nightclubs where she performs.

How do the clubs get around this? Very simply put, they are very strict with Debbie. She's allowed to go in the stage door and on the stage, but, unless it's a teen club, she is not permitted to be on the dance floor or anywhere in the main part of the club.

Debbie handles this with her usual ease. In those cases, she usually just performs and leaves the club. She looks at it this way: She's there to do a job, entertain and make the crowd happy. There's plenty of time later for her to have fun with her own crowd at some other place.

There are good things and bad things about being on the road. One of the good things is that it's energizing to appear in front of a live audience. The bad thing is that it's often lonely. Luckily, Debbie doesn't have that problem. Her sister, Karen, travels with her and does her sound engineering, and her mother, Diane, comes along as her manager.

The songwriting part simply comes naturally to Debbie. As far as arranging goes, she says she can simply *imagine* all the different instrumental parts when she composes.

Of course, she has always played around with multitrack recording, and now that she has a twelve track, soon to be twenty-four track, studio set up in her own house, she can do a lot of experimentation and keep playing it back until she gets the sound she's looking for.

So she can write and do arrangements and preproduction work right in her own home. Only after all that has been done does she invite her musician friends over and *then* play the songs. Debbie said it's really great when all the instruments come together and create the sound that she's been hearing in her head.

That's what creativity is all about. But it takes more than one person, and Debbie knows that. She may get an idea, hear it in her head and compose the song, but it takes her and the other musicians working together to make it come alive!

There was no question in anyone's mind that she could continue the success of her first album with her second, *Electric Youth*. It has the sound, the sound that clicks in the heads of her fans, and will probably sell many records.

Let's say you want to hear a big splashy ballad about heartbreak and longing. Well, you've got it with the first single on the album, "Lost in Your Eyes," as well as "Silence Speaks a Thousand Words" and "No More Rhyme."

"No More Rhyme," said Deb, "is about the need for 'rhythm' in a relationship." It has

At music station Hot 97's Radioathon in March 1989 with Diane Sawyer. Robin Platzer, Images

lines like: I always felt the rhythm/What happens when there's no more rhyme?

If you're looking for big-production "rock" tunes with great dance beats, then you'll love the title track, which is sort of an anthem to the future with this line: The next generation is electric!

"Who Loves Ya Baby?" and "We Could Be Together" are two more hot numbers. Each of these builds to a catchy and completely unstoppable chorus that will lodge in your brain and stay with you for days.

Those are just a few reasons why *Electric Youth* is such a smash. All of which proves that Debbie is one cool little pixie who can concoct remarkable catchy tunes.

In many ways, Debbie Gibson is a mixture. On one hand she is *not* your average eighteen-year-old. Her peers do not get triple-platinum albums before they get their driver's licenses. They do not headline at Radio City, are not invited on stage with Elton John and Billy Joel, and definitely do *not* have their high-school graduations videotaped for the nightly news. Also, average 18-year-olds hardly ever ask photographers to focus on the left sides of their faces because that's their best angle.

That's the professional part of the mixture. But on the other hand, Debbie *is* your average teenager who reads teen magazines and giggles at the mention of George Michael's name. She has no intention of letting success change her.

"When I was in school, I kept a low profile," recalls Debbie. "My friends think it's neat. When I come back from a trip, the first thing I do is get on the phone with them. You can tell the people who want to be your friends only because you're in the spotlight, because that's all they talk about. To me, a friend is someone you can call up even when you have no new news, and just talk."

She doesn't date much and usually prefers to go out in groups to the movies and such. "I'm not at the point where I want to be serious with anybody. The longest any boyfriend has lasted is three months. I'm not into older guys, either," she says. "I like to stick with my own age."

Debbie is often asked what is the craziest thing she has ever done. She doesn't even have to stop and think about it, so strongly is it etched in her memory. Debbie laughs as she recalls, "I was at the beach in Hollywood, Florida, where the *Hollywood Squares* was being taped. Mitch Gaylord was one of the guests on the show, and I'm crazy about him! I knew I couldn't be this close without seeing him. I tried to get tickets, but there weren't any left, so I went and hid behind a rock where they were taping the show. I waited *two hours* and finally, during a commercial break, I ran past the security guards, hopped over the dividers and ran right into the squares where the stars sit and asked, "Mitch, can I take a picture of you?"

Debbie continued, "Bizarre, right? Well, he let me, and I gave him my record! Now we're friends, and I've even been on his show!"

It's interesting to know that even though she's a star, Debbie can be a star-struck teenager just like everybody else.

She believes in acting your age, no matter what your age. She comments, "Adolescence is a time of life, distinct from childhood. Enjoying each stage of your life is what it's all about."

Unlike a lot of young stars, Debbie is trying to make sure she doesn't miss out on all the fun that comes with being a teenager.

Debbie's life has been spent in pursuit of her dream, and the years of dedication have turned her into a seasoned trooper.

Take a record-release party at the Hard Rock Cafe, for example. Gibson worked the room like a true pro, all the while surrounded by a video crew, photographers, record-company folks and a bodyguard. She talked with MTV's Julie Brown. And as the title song of *Electric Youth* pounded out over the PA system, she lip-synced a dance routine with two dancers from her band.

"I always knew that it wasn't enough just to make music or to get up on a stage," she explains. "I was brought up to believe in the idea of *work* going along with pleasure. So I know all about that."

The secret behind Debbie Gibson is that she has always had a goal. She has known since she was a little girl exactly what she wanted to be. And she went after it, knowing full well the hard work and dedication it required. She studied music, learned the classics, and did something toward her musical career *every day*. Always eager to learn and always open to new ideas and alert to situations that could be turned into song, Debbie remained true to her single-minded purpose—her dream.

And it has paid off. The dream has become a reality. Along the way, she has learned an important lesson. The work part never goes away. That's fine with Debbie, because she *loves* her work!

What's Next?

What does the future hold for Debbie Gibson? Too often people who score such awesome success at such an early age find their popularity fading by the time they are in their twenties. Their names wind up in one of those "whatever became of...?" books, or else they become a question in a trivia game. Luck and talent—it takes both. Luck to make it, and talent to stay there.

As cohost of the 1989 American Music Awards, Debbie rehearses with executive producer Dick Clark at Los Angeles' Shrine Auditorium. AP/Wide World Photos

A lot of people are betting that Debbie Gibson will be around for a long time to come. As her voice matures, so will her writing. Her plan is to reflect the age in which she is living, so her songs will become songs to fit whatever age she happens to be. Her fans will grow with her. As she matures, they will mature, too. Their interests will change, and so will Debbie's.

Her career, if all goes according to plan, will be a continuing process. Growing as she grows, maturing as she matures, so that with each passing year her music will attain new depth, and new meaning for the legion of fans whose hearts she has won.

So far, everything is on track. "Lost in Your Eyes" is a tremendous hit. Debbie was cohost of the American Music Awards. She has a "major video" out and, of course, there's always the movies and that screenplay she's been writing.

"It's basically a teen movie with a different twist," she said. She refuses to give out the story line, because, "Remember when there were, like, four movies out with fathers and sons changing bodies? Well, I always thought somebody must have leaked that idea somewhere, and I don't want that to happen to mine!"

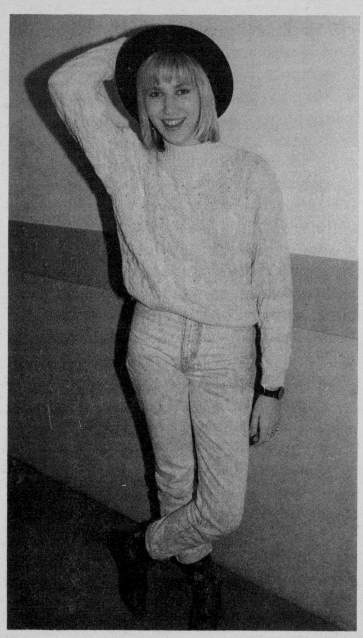

The future is in the hands of youth, and Debbie seems to be lead-ing the way. Judie Burstein/Photoreporters

So Debbie is not standing still. She's not one to sit back and rest on her laurels. She seems to sense that the only way to stay on top is to stay on top of what's happening in the music world and in the world of her fans.

Her platinum success has not been without its price. Now an ominous bodyguard attends her public appearances (not when she goes shopping with her friends). Her family has had to change their phone number a few times, but now it is unlisted. "You get weird phone calls from people you've never met saying, 'Don't you remember me?' so it can get pretty spooky."

Overall, of course, she couldn't be happier with her life. Debbie is a true careerist. Hers is the sound of young America, full of life and excitement about the future.

The future is in the hands of young America. Whatever they (the fans) do with it, Debbie will be right there with them, leading the way and responding to their needs, because more than being a star, Debbie Gibson is one of them!

Hard work certainly has paid off for Debbie, who has been performing since she was three years old. AP/Wide World Photos

Vital Statistics

BIRTHPLACE: Brooklyn, New York.
BIRTHDAY: August 31, 1970.
NAMES SHE'LL ANSWER TO: Deborah, Debs, The Gibber, Denbie.
FAVORITE EXPRESSIONS: "We're off like a dirty shirt." "What you are is God's gift to you—what you *become* is your gift to God."
LIKES: Billy Joel, children, laughing, pennies, 1950s, teddy bears, chocolate shakes, stupid jokes, hotel pianos, the movies *Grease* and *Dirty Dancing*, jeans, hats, baggy jackets, sweaters and shirts,

Madonna, "man-in-the-street" jewelry, New York City, being a teenager and Grandma's football meatballs.

DISLIKES: Shoelaces, auto-revolving doors, $20 hamburgers, airplane food, rumors, misquotes, feedback, pushy guys, phony people, nosy people, income questions, the thought of being in an elevator with the Fat Boys, being wrong and the word "can't."

AMBITION: To win a Grammy, the ultimate symbol of music-biz respectability. To get married and have children. To never sacrifice her beliefs—no matter what the consequence, no matter what the reward.